THE MICROWAVE
Shakespeare

Other titles in the series

THE TRAGEDY OF
MACBETH

Ransom

Macbeth
Published by Ransom Publishing Ltd.
Unit 7, Brocklands Farm, West Meon, Hampshire GU32 1JN, UK
www.ransom.co.uk

ISBN   978 178591 338 9
First published in 2019

CONTENTS

WHERE

Scotland. At the time of the play, Scotland and England were separate countries.

SCOTLAND

Birnam Wood

Dunsinane

ENGLAND

WALES

WHEN

The events in the play take place some time in the past. There *was* a real king of the Scots called Macbeth; he died in 1057.

The play itself was written in about 1605.

At this time, people thought that kings were chosen by God. So trying to change who was king was a really bad sin.

The full title of the play is *The Tragedy of Macbeth*.

WHO

Duncan, King of the Scots – a good king

Malcolm – his son
Donalbain – his other son

Malcolm   King Duncan   Donalbain

The king's noblemen

Macbeth, Thane of Glamis
Lady Macbeth – his wife

Macbeth   Lady Macbeth   Banquo

Banquo – loyal to King Duncan
Fleance – Banquo's son

Ross – loyal to King Duncan
Angus – loyal to King Duncan
Lennox – loyal to King Duncan
Macduff, Thane of Fife – loyal to King Duncan

Macdonwald – traitor to King Duncan

Thane of Cawdor – traitor to King Duncan

Old Siward – English general
Young Siward – his son

The three witches – hags with supernatural powers. They may not be human

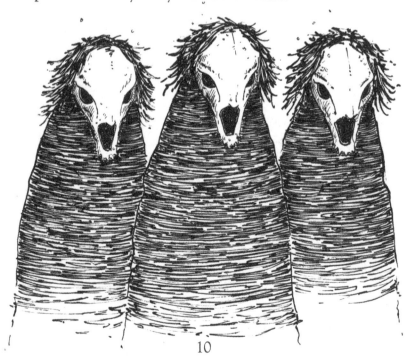

HELPFUL NOTE

All the spoken words in this book that are in italics, *'like this'*, are actual words taken from Shakespeare's play. They are spoken by one of the actors in the play.

The Globe Theatre. Above is a reconstruction of the original Globe Theatre, which is in London. Below is a cross-section of the original theatre, which was built in 1599.

Shakespeare's plays were performed at this theatre. When you read this book, just imagine standing in the crowd, in front of this stage, watching the play.

ONE

The three witches are gathered at some deserted, nasty place. There's thunder and lightning. You can feel the evil building up.

'*Fair is foul, and foul is fair:*
Hover through the fog and filthy air.'

You can almost taste the evil.

'*When shall we three meet again?*' they ask.

'*When the battle's lost and won,*'

(whatever that means). Then, they say, they will meet with **Macbeth**.

Meanwhile, a great battle is raging. The

forces of Norway and Ireland, led by the traitors **Macdonwald** and the **Thane of Cawdor**, are attacking the Scots forces.

Meanwhile, **Duncan**, **King of the Scots**, is at his camp, listening to reports coming in from the battle. He hears that his brave generals **Macbeth, Thane of Glamis**, and **Banquo** both fought bravely in the midst of battle. Macbeth thrust his sword into the stomach of the traitor Macdonwald (definitely a bad guy) and sawed his way up to Macdonwald's jawbone. Then he cut off Macdonwald's head and fixed it on the battlements. (That told *him*!)

The Norwegian lord, with fresh arms and fresh soldiers, started a new attack on the Scots, but Macbeth and Banquo stood tall. Back-to-back they fought, slashing and stabbing the enemy!

The reek of blood was in their nostrils as the Scots claimed victory in the battle.

Duncan is pleased. Macbeth has defended Scotland and has saved him and his sons from death.

After the battle, the three witches meet again.

'*Where hast thou been, sister?*'

'*Killing swine.*'

(They are *such* nice people!)

Macbeth and Banquo are trudging wearily across the heath, (it has been a tough day at the ~~office~~ battle), when they come across the witches.

Banquo stops suddenly.

'What are these things?' he asks. 'They look like women, but they have beards. Are they of this earth?'

The witches each greet Macbeth:

'*All hail, Macbeth! hail to thee, thane of Glamis!*'

'*All hail, Macbeth, hail to thee, thane of Cawdor!*'

'All hail, Macbeth, *thou shalt be king hereafter!*'

Macbeth is stunned. He is Thane of Glamis, sure, but he is not Thane of Cawdor – and definitely not King of Scotland. Cawdor and Duncan are both alive and well. What are these hags talking about?

Banquo then asks the witches to greet him, too. The witches tell him that he shall be father to a line of kings, but that he shall not be a king himself.

Then they tell him that he shall be:

'*Lesser than Macbeth, and greater.*'

16

'Not so happy, yet much happier.'

Then the witches vanish into thin air.

Just as Banquo and Macbeth are talking about what the witches had said, the Thanes **Ross** and **Angus** appear, sent by the king.

Ross tells Macbeth that the traitor the Thane of Cawdor is to be executed, by the king's orders. On top of that, the king was so impressed by Macbeth's bravery on the battlefield that he is giving him Cawdor's title.

One of the witches' predictions has just come true. [*Woooooo … spooky!*]

Macbeth starts thinking about how the witches greeted him …

'*If chance will have me king, why, chance may crown me,*

Without my stir,' he says.

The witches got the first bit right … perhaps he *will* become king, without even trying, without having to … there will be no need to … you know … kill the king.

Back at HQ, King Duncan greets Macbeth and Banquo. He praises them and says he will spend the coming night at Macbeth's castle at Inverness. (Having the king for a sleepover was a great privilege in those days.)

Duncan also names his son **Malcolm** as his heir and gives him the title Prince of Cumberland.

Macbeth is trying hard not to grind his

teeth at this news. He hopes no one will find out about his recent 'black and deep desires'.

Macbeth sends a message to his wife, **Lady Macbeth**, who is at home at Inverness Castle. He tells her that the king is coming to stay for the night – and he also tells her about the meeting with the witches, and what they said.

Back home in Inverness, Lady Macbeth reads her husband's message. It tells her the 'wonderful' story of the meeting with the witches.

But in her head, another wonderful story is already unfolding. It is a story of Queen Macbeth, dressed in beautiful gowns, everyone hanging on her every word. No more cold, wet castle in the middle of nowhere! Her husband shall be king of

Scotland and she shall be queen. They will make it happen. They will kill King Duncan.

But Lady Macbeth isn't sure that her husband is up to the job of killing Duncan. Macbeth, she thinks, is too weak, *'too full o' the milk of human kindness.'*

Then a messenger arrives, telling her that Macbeth and Duncan are already on their way.

Lady Macbeth makes her decision. There is a job to do – and she needs to be up for it. Duncan will be killed.

'Now,' she says to herself, *'fill me from the crown to the toe top-full*

Of direst cruelty! make thick my blood.' In other words, make me cruel enough to do this. And don't let me regret it afterwards.

Then Macbeth arrives. Lady Macbeth greets him: 'My great Thane of Glamis! My great Thane of Cawdor! You are destined to be even greater – I can feel it!'

Macbeth tells her that Duncan is staying with them that night.

'And he will never leave!' she says. 'We must sort him out tonight.'

She tells Macbeth he must, '*look like the innocent flower,*

But be the serpent under 't.'

'Hang on,' says Macbeth. He wants to talk about it. His wife is going a bit fast for him!

'No!' she says. '*Leave all the rest to me.*'

'This is a pleasant castle,' Duncan says, as he rides up to the Macbeth household. (Little does he know!)

Banquo agrees. (He always agrees with the king. Banquo is an honest man and he believes that the king always knows best.)

'And,' says Duncan, 'here comes our honoured hostess!'

Duncan thanks Lady Macbeth for her trouble. She tells him that four times as much trouble would not repay the honour he does her. She smiles and smiles until her face aches. (It's hard work plotting murders.)

But Macbeth is having second thoughts.

'What shall I do?' he asks himself. 'If I kill Duncan, things will happen in this life and in the next. I'm pretty sure you don't go to Heaven if you've killed your king. Also, I am a relation of his – and I'm his subject. He's my guest tonight, too. Plus, he is a really nice king and a good old man. I should be the one to protect him, not cut him myself.'

'But then again,' he tells himself, 'I do want to be king … '

Just then Lady Macbeth comes in, looking for her husband. 'What are you playing at? The king has been asking for you!'

'Look,' says her lily-livered husband, *We will proceed no further in this business.* Everything is fine as it is. Everyone likes me and I have a new title. I'm not going to do it.'

'You are just a coward,' says his wife. 'When you dared to do it, you were a man. Now you are nothing! The timing is perfect: the king is here and he's just asking for it!

'I have fed my baby at my breast. I would rather have taken it off the nipple and dashed out its brains while it was smiling at me, than be the kind of coward you are!'

There's no messing with Lady Macbeth when she's in this kind of mood!

'What if something goes wrong?' Macbeth asks.

'Nothing will go wrong!' says Lady Macbeth.

She has an answer for everything.

'*Screw your courage to the sticking-place,*

And we'll not fail,' she tells him. 'I'll drug his servants. He's had a busy day, so he will sleep well. Then we'll kill him and smear blood on the grooms' clothes, so they get the blame. We will cry and roar our grief when they find him, as if we loved the old fool!'

(The grooms are the king's servants.)

'OK,' Macbeth decides. 'Let's do it! *False face must hide what the false heart doth know.*'

TWO

That night, Banquo and his son **Fleance** are taking it in turns to patrol the castle courtyard. Banquo is feeling jumpy – it's been quite a day!

Then Macbeth turns up. Banquo is pleased to see him. He tells Macbeth that the king has gone to bed happy. And Duncan has been generous to Macbeth's people. He even gave Lady Macbeth a diamond as a gift.

Then Banquo and Fleance leave; Macbeth is alone.

Suddenly, Macbeth has a vision of a bloody dagger floating in the air in front of him. It is dripping thick clots of blood. His heart nearly leaps out of his chest.

'*Is this a dagger which I see before me?*'

He grabs at it. It's gone!

'A *dagger of the mind?*'

Is it real? No! Yes! It's back!

'I must be going mad!'

It seems to Macbeth that in the darkness, nature is dead. Evil is visiting the dreams of those who sleep. The stones themselves seem to shout out: 'Macbeth is here now! He is the murderer!'

At last the bell rings. It is the signal. Macbeth goes to kill his king!

Lady Macbeth has placed the daggers in the king's room, ready for her husband. She thinks to herself that she would have done the killing herself, except that the sleeping king looked like her father.

Somehow, she couldn't do it.

His hands dripping with the king's blood, Macbeth tells his wife that it is done.

She snaps at him. *'Why did you bring these daggers from the place?*

They must lie there: go carry them; and smear

The sleepy grooms with blood.'

Macbeth won't go back with the daggers – he can't look at the dead king. He feels as if he will never sleep again – a picture of Duncan is fixed on the insides of his eyelids.

So Lady Macbeth returns the daggers to the king's room.

There is knocking inside the castle, and Macbeth nearly jumps out of his skin. How can he wash the blood from his hands? There is too much gore. The blood is a witness to his killing. The thick blood would turn an ocean into a bloody sea.

Lady Macbeth rushes back in. 'Come and wash! My hands are the same! *A little water clears us of this deed.'*

The knocking continues. 'Oh,' Macbeth groans, 'listen to that knocking! Duncan, I wish you could hear it!'

(Is Macbeth beginning to hear things too?) His wife drags him away.

The knocking continues. It is a knocking on the main castle door. The gate-keeper is still drunk from the night before, but he manages to open up.

'Late night?' **Macduff, Thane of Fife** asks him. (He and the nobleman **Lennox** have arrived at the castle to give the king an early morning call.)

'Sir,' the gate-keeper says, 'I had lots to drink, which causes three things: a red nose, sleep, and the need to pee. It also causes you to want a woman, but if you're drunk, you can't do anything once you've found her!'

Macbeth arrives to greet Lennox and Macduff. While Macbeth chats with Lennox, Macduff goes to wake the king.

He's back pretty quickly.

'O, *horror, horror, horror!*'

Looks like he's found the king.

Macduff makes a lot of noise, calling

Banquo and Duncan's sons, **Donalbain** and
Malcolm, to see for themselves. He also
tells Lennox and Macbeth – and Lady
Macbeth, who turns up asking sweetly what
all the fuss is about.

'Oh, gentle lady! The king has been
murdered!'

'What, in our house?' Lady Macbeth asks.

'Is she for real?' thinks Banquo. 'It would
be a terrible thing wherever it happens!'

Macbeth then tells Malcolm and Donalbain

that their father is dead. He tells them it looks as though the grooms killed him.

Macbeth then goes straight into the king's bedroom and kills the two grooms. He comes back out and admits what he's just done. He killed them in anger, he says, out of *violent love* for Duncan. (Yeah, right.)

Before anyone can question Macbeth more closely, Lady Macbeth pretends to faint, and calls for help.

Donalbain and Malcolm may be young, but they aren't daft. They quickly put two and two together.

'Let's find somewhere safe, quickly,' Donalbain says to his brother Malcolm.

'I'm going to England straight away,' says Malcolm.

'I'll be in Ireland. We'll be safer apart,' says Donalbain.

In other words, they think it wasn't the servants who did it!

Everyone decides to meet later, once they have had time to think.

Ross is talking to an old man outside Macbeth's castle. Strange things have been happening. It is daytime, but darkness lies across Scotland.

Only last week, the old man says, he saw a falcon killed by a little owl.

Ross says the king's horses broke out of their stables and then started to eat each other!

The two of them are amazed – everything is strange – fair is foul and foul is fair.

Then Macduff joins them. He tells Ross and the old man that the king's sons, Malcolm and Donalbain, have fled. It looks as though they were guilty of their father's murder in some way.

Macduff then says that it's most likely that Macbeth will now be made King of Scotland. In fact, he has already gone to Scone to be crowned. (Scone is a place, not something you eat! Just saying.)

THREE

Banquo is muttering to himself. He can see that Macbeth has now got everything *'the weird women'* predicted: Glamis, Cawdor *and* king. Deep down, Banquo thinks it's possible that Macbeth murdered Duncan, just to get what he wanted.

And perhaps, thinks Banquo, the witches' prediction will come true for him as well. Maybe his son Fleance will become a king …

Macbeth invites Banquo to a feast at his castle that evening. But first, Banquo is going out riding that afternoon with his son. Macbeth is careful to find out exactly where they will be riding.

After Banquo has gone, Macbeth has a good think. He knows that the witches' predictions came true for him – and he knows that Banquo knows. And Banquo knows that Macbeth knows that Banquo knows …

Can Macbeth trust Banquo?

Macbeth also wants to make sure that Banquo's sons will never be kings. The witch's prediction for Banquo *must not* come true.

Macbeth calls in two murderers and tells them that Banquo has caused them harm. They must kill him.

'And Fleance, his son,' Macbeth tells them. 'Make sure you kill him too!'

(The murderers have no real choice anyway – they can't disobey orders from their king!) Macbeth tells them when and where to do the dirty deed – and he says it must be done today.

Later in the day, before the feast, Lady Macbeth is talking to her husband.

'*Be bright and jovial among your guests to-night.*'

'I feel like my mind is full of scorpions whilst Banquo and Fleance live. But it will be sorted!' he says.

'What are you going to do?' asks Lady Macbeth.

'You don't need to know, dear lady, you don't need to know!' Macbeth taps his nose.

Macbeth sends another murderer to watch the other two. Macbeth has to be sure that Banquo and Fleance are killed!

Banquo is walking alongside his horse when the murderers attack him. As he dies, Banquo shouts, '*O, treachery! Fly, good Fleance, fly, fly, fly!*'

Fleance runs for his life and escapes.

Meanwhile, Macbeth is in the warm, sitting down to his feast with all the lords and ladies.

One of the murderers beckons him to the door and gives him the news.

'My lord, he's dead. I cut his throat.'

'And Fleance?'

Macbeth feels cold as he hears the murderer's words: 'He got away.'

Macbeth goes back to the feast, but now there is nowhere for him to sit.

Lennox says, 'Here's an empty seat' – but as Macbeth looks, he sees the ghost of Banquo sitting there. Macbeth's blood runs cold. It's clear that nobody except Macbeth can see the ghost.

The ghost shakes its bloody head at Macbeth.

'*Thou canst not say I did it: never shake Thy gory locks at me,*' Macbeth shouts at the ghost, as he backs away.

Lady Macbeth tries to gloss over Macbeth's sudden strange behaviour.

'The King's not well. He's had this illness since he was a boy. Ignore him – he'll be OK soon!'

She turns to Macbeth. 'Man up! There's nobody there. *Why do you make such faces? You're just looking at a stool!*'

The ghost disappears and Macbeth tries to act as if everything is normal.

'I'm sorry! Come on, let's have a drink. Let's drink to Banquo! I wish he had made it here this evening! To Banquo!'

But then the ghost appears again – and Macbeth loses control again.

'*Quit my sight! … thy blood is cold.* You glare at me with zombie eyes!'

Then the ghost vanishes again.

The lords and ladies at the feast decide that their new king is not quite all there. They all make their apologies and leave. Now just Macbeth and Lady Macbeth are left there.

Suddenly a thought crosses Macbeth's mind. Where is Macduff? He was invited to the feast. Why didn't he turn up?

'Does he defy me? … Tomorrow I will see those weird sisters … I am thinking … I have spilled so much blood, I might as well wade through the stuff to the other side. Hmmm … Macduff … '

Lady Macbeth almost doesn't recognise her husband any more. He makes no sense.

'Sleep, my lord, you need to get some sleep.'

'What I need is to get used to this. *We are yet but young in deed.*'

'Get used to killing,' is what Macbeth is thinking. There is more killing to be done.

Meanwhile, Lennox has been doing some thinking himself.

'Duncan was envied by Macbeth, then he died. Banquo went out riding late, and he died. Did Malcolm and Donalbain kill their father? Did Fleance kill his father? I don't think so! Something else is going on.'

Meanwhile, Macduff has gone to England to ask the English king for help. Lennox decides to send a message to Macduff:

'Be very, very careful!'

FOUR

The witches are in a cave, brewing up a spell in their cauldron. They dance round and round:

> *'Double, double toil and trouble;*
> *Fire burn and cauldron bubble …*
> *Cool it with a baboon's blood,*
> *Then the charm is firm and good.'*

Then one says:

> *'By the pricking of my thumbs,*
> *Something wicked this way comes.'*

And at that moment Macbeth walks in. He tells the witches he needs some answers!

They agree to answer – and a head

without a body suddenly appears in front of Macbeth. It speaks:

'*Macbeth! Macbeth! Macbeth! beware Macduff.*'

Then a child covered in blood appears. It also speaks:

'Nobody born of woman will hurt Macbeth!'

'Well,' thinks Macbeth, 'if that's true, then nobody can kill me, because everybody has a mother! Result!'

So if he can't be killed, he doesn't really need to worry about Macduff. 'But then,' Macbeth thinks, 'it's probably best to kill Macduff anyway, just to make sure.'

Finally a child wearing a crown and holding a tree, appears in front of Macbeth. It also speaks:

'Macbeth will not be beaten until Birnam Wood comes to Dunsinane Hill.'

'Huh! Well, a wood cannot move,' thinks Macbeth. 'So it looks like I will never be defeated. More good news!'

Then Macbeth asks the witches whether Banquo's heirs will ever become king (as they predicted). Eight kings then appear in a line, followed by Banquo, who is smiling and pointing at the kings. The eighth king is carrying a mirror showing even more kings.

The witches speak:

'Why are you surprised? We told you so! We told you so!'

Then, pop! They are gone.

Macbeth learns that Macduff has fled to

England. In that case, Macbeth decides, he will send soldiers to Macduff's castle to kill his wife, his children, his servants … and anyone else who happens to be around.

At Macduff's castle, Lady Macduff is frantic. Why did her husband leave Scotland? What was he thinking? Now they are all alone and defenceless.

Then Macbeth's murderers arrive – and Macduff's family is murdered.

In England, Macduff and Malcolm are having a bit of a chat. They know they should be loyal to King Macbeth, but they fear him and his cruelty.

Macduff and Malcolm each try to find out what the other is thinking. They test each other with gentle comments and decide that they can trust each other. They begin to plan.

Old Siward, the English general, has an army of ten thousand men. He will join them, with his army, in fighting against Macbeth, if they can agree to march on Scotland together.

The King of England supports Malcolm and he is a holy, saint-like king. It will be a good fight! They must win and get their beloved Scotland back on track!

Just then, Ross turns up.

'How are my wife and children?' Macduff asks him. Ross tries to tell him what has happened to his family, but he can't.

'They were well at peace when I did leave 'em,' Ross says.

Malcolm is telling Ross about their plans to invade Scotland, but Macduff is thinking about Ross' answer. Enjoying peace and quiet, he thinks, or resting in peace? Oh no!

So Macduff forces Ross to tell him the truth about his family.

Ross tells him, *'Your castle is surprised; your wife and babes*

Savagely slaughter'd …
Wife, children, servants, all
That could be found.'

Macduff is half-mad with grief and is set on killing Macbeth. Malcolm tells Macduff to turn his grief into anger:

'Let's make us medicines of our great revenge,

To cure this deadly grief.'

The three noblemen get ready for the march to Scotland.

FIVE

At the king's palace at Dunsinane, Lady Macbeth has lost her mind.

The doctor and the nurse listen as she sleepwalks in a trance, babbling on about dead people: Duncan, Banquo, Lady Macduff, her children; so many deaths.

'Here's a spot …

Out, damned spot! out, I say!'

She is trying to wash the blood from her hands, but she cannot get rid of it. She can't get rid of the smell of the blood either.

The doctor tells the nurse to keep Lady Macbeth from harm: she is quite, quite mad.

Meanwhile, the Scots rebels and the English troops, led by Malcolm, Macduff and Siward, have arranged to meet at Birnam Wood, a forest not far from the Scots king's palace at Dunsinane.

(Can you feel it all coming together, just as the witches said it would?)

In his palace at Dunsinane, Macbeth is getting reports of the massive enemy army that is gathering. He's not in a good mood and shouts at the servants:

'The devil damn thee black, thou cream-faced loon!'

But Macbeth knows he's safe: Malcolm was 'born of a woman' and Birnam Wood cannot move to his palace (forests can't walk). So, as the witches predicted, he cannot be harmed. Macbeth is going to win!

The English soldiers meet the Scots at Birnam Wood. Then Malcolm has a bright idea. Every soldier should carry a large branch of a tree as camouflage, so Macbeth and his forces can't see how big the advancing army is.

(Got it yet? It will look just as if the wood is moving!)

As Macbeth prepares for battle, he learns that the queen – Lady Macbeth – has died. He doesn't even ask how she died. (We find out at the very end of the play that she probably killed herself.)

'She should have left it until I had time to be sad,' he yells.

Then he thinks about how small a life is, in the big scale of things:

'Life's but a walking shadow, a poor player [actor]
That struts and frets his hour upon the stage
And then is heard no more: it is a tale
Told by an idiot, full of sound and fury,
Signifying nothing.'

Then a messenger comes in.

'My lord, don't be angry, but … I'm sure I saw Birnam Wood begin to move.'

More bad news. It's all happening now!

Macbeth has another good shout:

'If you are lying, you are going to hang on one of those trees yourself.'

Macbeth goes out to fight – and the battle begins.

Macbeth is cornered, but it's OK: nobody can kill him, remember? He fights with **Young Siward** and stabs him straight through with his sword.

'Ha!' thinks Macbeth, 'No one born of woman can kill me!'

Macbeth is laughing like a madman when Macduff finds him.

'Get away!' Macbeth shouts, 'I have killed all your family. I've killed enough Macduffs – boring! – I'm not killing you!'

Now Macduff has no doubt. He must kill Macbeth, or the ghosts of his poor dead wife and his little murdered children will haunt him.

'*Tyrant, show thy face!*' Macduff shouts.
If thou be'st slain and with no stroke of mine,
My wife and children's ghosts will haunt me still.'

'You are wasting your time,' Macbeth gloats. '*I bear a charmed life.* No man born of a woman can kill me! Loser!'

Suddenly Macduff has an 'Aha!' moment. He realises that this is his destiny. Because Macduff was not 'born of a woman'. Rather, he was taken out of his mother's womb by a surgeon. (It's called a Caesarean section – look it up!)

Macduff gleefully tells Macbeth that fact. 'Surrender, coward!' he tells Macbeth.

'*I will not yield …*

Though Birnam wood be come to *Dunsinane,*

And thou opposed, being of no woman born, Yet I will try the last. '

Macbeth will fight to the end.

He and Macduff fight – and Macbeth is killed.

The battle – and Macbeth's reign as king – is over.

Later that day, Macduff enters, carrying Macbeth's head on a spear.

Everybody hails Malcolm, good Malcolm, as the new king of Scotland.

THE END

What's the play about?

This bloody play is about greed, the lust for power and how people can become corrupted. Macbeth did not murder because he liked to murder. He murdered in order to get what he wanted.

The play is about **greed**.

It's about how **ambition** can make us act badly.

It's about how bad can follow bad.
* For Macbeth, one murder leads to many. He only kills Banquo and Macduff's family because he's afraid they will tell people that he killed Duncan.

It's about **making choices** in our lives.

✱ Banquo and Macbeth begin the play at the same rank, but they make different choices in the play. Banquo does not kill to make his son king; that is *his* choice.

At first Macbeth is not sure if he should kill Duncan, but Lady Macbeth is sure: Duncan must be killed. So Macbeth, too, makes his choice. He kills to make the witches' prediction come true.

What are the main themes in the play?

Ambition – (especially for Macbeth and Lady Macbeth). Both are tempted by the idea that Macbeth will become king. At first, Macbeth has some doubts, but Lady Macbeth has none: they will kill Duncan. She even thinks her husband is a coward.

Remember that the witches spoke to Banquo too. Did he do anything to make their predictions about him come true?

Evil – Macbeth's search for power leads to evil thoughts and evil deeds.

The supernatural – Are there mysterious forces controlling what happens to us in our lives? Or do we decide what happens to us?

The three witches (who may not be

human) seem to be able to predict the future, and the play is full of other strange things happening.

In Shakespeare's time many people believed that supernatural forces controlled their lives.

Reality – Many times in the play people are not sure what is real. They 'see' things that they imagine: Macbeth 'sees' a dagger in front of him, and later he 'sees' the dead Banquo. Lady Macbeth 'sees' blood on her hands and she cannot get rid of it.

Their confusion about reality makes them paranoid.

Loyalty – Banquo and other lords are loyal to King Duncan. Cawdor is killed because he is not loyal to the king. Macbeth is not loyal to Duncan, yet he expects his own servants to be loyal to him.

Guilt – Macbeth regrets killing Duncan

(he feels guilty). This guilt makes him fall into madness.

Lady Macbeth seems to feel no guilt, but eventually her guilt also drives her mad (and kills her).

Shakespeare's words

Shakespeare loved to make up his own words and phrases. Many of them are now part of everyday English.

He uses language in this play in different ways and for different reasons.

Sometimes Shakespeare wants his characters to say a lot with only a **few words**.

✳ The witches tell Banquo that compared to Macbeth he will be:

'Lesser than Macbeth, and greater.'
'Not so happy, yet much happier.'

This says exactly what happens to Banquo in the play: he is lesser than Macbeth (he's not a king), but he is greater too (not a bad person/killer); he is not so happy (again, not a king), but happier (he does not feel guilty about his actions.)

Sometimes Shakespeare wants his characters to say things which are not very clear. He wants them to say **ambiguous** things.

* At the beginning of the play the witches say:
  'Fair is foul and foul is fair.'

  They could have said 'everything is mixed up,' or 'things are the opposite of what they seem,' but *'Fair is foul and foul is fair'* isn't so clear. We can spot many things in the play where bad is good and good is bad: Macbeth is king (good), but he is a bad person. And if the witches are evil, would they think that bad is good?

Sometimes Shakespeare wants to put **strong images** in our minds.

* When Lady Macbeth and Macbeth are talking about killing Duncan, Lady

Macbeth tells her husband to:

> 'Screw your courage to the
> sticking-place
> And we'll not fail.'

It's just a lovely way of saying, 'Be strong. We can do this.'

Sometimes Shakespeare wants us to know what his characters are **thinking**.

* Macbeth (and Lady Macbeth) often talk to themselves, with little speeches that nobody is meant to hear. (This kind of speech is called a **soliloquy**.) It is a way of letting the audience know what the person is thinking.

   So when Macbeth is alone in the castle, he sees a bloody dagger appear in front of him. We need him to give his speech, starting:

   > 'Is this a dagger which I see before me?'

   so that we know that he is, just maybe, starting to go mad.